Fighter Pilots

By Antony Loveless

CRABTREE
Publishing Company
www.crabtreebooks.com

The World's MOST DANGEROUS Jobs

Editors: Mark Sachner, Adrianna Morganelli
Editorial director: Kathy Middleton
Proofreader: Redbud Editorial
Production coordinator: Margaret Salter
Prepress technician: Margaret Salter
Project director: Ruth Owen
Designer: Elaine Wilkinson
Cover design: Alix Wood

Photo credits:
Black Rat Media: cover (bottom), pages 6, 9, 11, 12,
    16 (main), 22, 23, 24–25, 26
Corbis: Alain Nogues: page 7
Department of Defense: cover (top), page 1, 5, 8,
    14,14–15, 16 (inset), 17, 19, 21, 27, 28–29

COVER STORY

◄ **COVER (top) – Two United States Air Force (USAF) F-22 Raptors fly in formation as they undertake a training sortie (mission).**

◄ **COVER (bottom) – A pilot's face shows the effects of G-force while flying a Harrier Jump Jet.**

PAGE 1 – Two Royal Air Force (RAF) fighter pilots stand in front of their Tornado F3 fighter jet prior to a sortie (a flying mission).

Library and Archives Canada Cataloguing in Publication

Loveless, Antony
    Fighter pilots / Antony Loveless.

(The world's most dangerous jobs)
Includes index.
ISBN 978-0-7787-5096-3 (bound).--ISBN 978-0-7787-5110-6 (pbk.)

    1. Fighter pilots--Juvenile literature. 2. Fighter plane combat--
Juvenile literature. 3. Fighter planes--Juvenile literature. I. Title. II.
Series: World's most dangerous jobs

UG631.L695 2009   j623.74'64   C2009-903229-5

Library of Congress Cataloging-in-Publication Data

Loveless, Antony.
    Fighter pilots / Antony Loveless.
        p. cm. -- (The world's most dangerous jobs)
    Includes index.
    ISBN 978-0-7787-5096-3 (reinforced lib. bdg. : alk. paper)
-- ISBN 978-0-7787-5110-6 (pbk. : alk. paper)
    1. Fighter pilots--Juvenile literature. 2. Aeronautics, Military--Juvenile
literature. 3. Airplanes--Piloting--Juvenile literature. 4. Airplanes, Military--
Juvenile literature. I. Title.

    UG631.L68 2009
    623.74'64--dc22
                                              2009021570

Published by CRABTREE PUBLISHING COMPANY in 2010

Published in Canada
Crabtree Publishing
616 Welland Ave.
St. Catharines, ON
L2M 5V6

Published in the United States
Crabtree Publishing
PMB16A
350 Fifth Ave., Suite 3308
New York, NY 10118

Published in the United Kingdom
Crabtree Publishing
Lorna House, Suite 3.03, Lorna Road
Hove, East Sussex, UK
BN3 3EL

Published in Australia
Crabtree Publishing
386 Mt. Alexander Rd.
Ascot Vale (Melbourne)
VIC 3032

CONTENTS

Fighter Pilot 4

The Dangers 6

Training Fighter Pilots 8

G-force 10

Low-Level Flying 12

Raptors and Typhoons 14

Harriers and F-16s 16

Air-to-Air Refueling 18

A Fighter Pilot's Day 20

Quick Reaction Alert 22

QRA In Action 24

In Action 26

Danger Close 28

It's a Fact! 30

Glossary 31

Index 32

FIGHTER PILOT

In today's world, most people do not take part in dangerous activities during their day at work. They sit at desks in offices, or they work in shops and factories. For some people, however, facing danger is very much part of their everyday working life.

Fighter pilots go to work each day to fight for us and to protect us. These brave men and women risk their own lives to do one of the world's most dangerous jobs.

Fighter pilots are an important part of any country's military force. They fly some of the most complicated and advanced aircraft in the world.

> "Learning to fly jets is only half the battle. Each fighter jet is a weapons platform. A fighter pilot must be better than his or her rival when using the plane's weapons. There are no second places in aerial combat!"
>
> **Megan, United States Air Force (USAF) F-16 Pilot**

Fighter pilots attack the enemy from the air and protect their own land forces from airborne attack. They stop enemy planes from flying by bombing them on the ground. They also engage with them in the air and shoot them down. Fighter pilots do their job with the knowledge that they could be attacked from the ground or by an enemy plane at any time.

Today, the danger of a terrorist attack from the air is all too real. If terrorists are in control of a plane, a nation's air force may order its fighter pilots to shoot down the plane.

▲ A Harrier GR9 deploys flares during a combat patrol over Afghanistan. The flares burn hotter than the Harrier's engine. If the enemy fires heat-seeking missiles at the plane, the heat of the flares will throw the missiles off course.

THE DANGERS

Combat flying is very dangerous, but fighter pilots face many other dangers, too.

Flying fast jets means the pilots experience high levels of **G-force**. This is the force you feel on your body when you are racing downhill on a rollercoaster. The G-force on a rollercoaster is about 3g. Fighter pilots can experience G-forces that are much higher. In extreme cases, pulling "high g" (up to 9g) can cause a pilot to black out and crash.

Fighter jets can have mechanical failures at high speeds. If the plane is in trouble and is headed for a crash, the fighter pilot is left with one last way to escape—ejecting.

Ejector seat

▼ The crew of a UK Royal Air Force (RAF) Tornado F3 prepares for a sortie (training mission).

"We sit on an ejector seat. If we have to abandon our aircraft we pull a lever between our legs. This sets off a chain of events. Within a second, the canopy above us is blown apart by a small explosive charge. Then, small rockets inside the seat propel the seat out of the aircraft. The seat contains a parachute that opens automatically, so we slowly descend to Earth. The whole process takes less than four seconds!

The real horror is that in combat you might be shot down or have to eject over enemy territory. If you survive, you can expect to be hunted down by enemy forces. That's when the real challenge begins—evading capture until you are rescued! Enemy forces will want to interrogate you, torture you, or even kill you."

Aaron, USAF F-22 Pilot

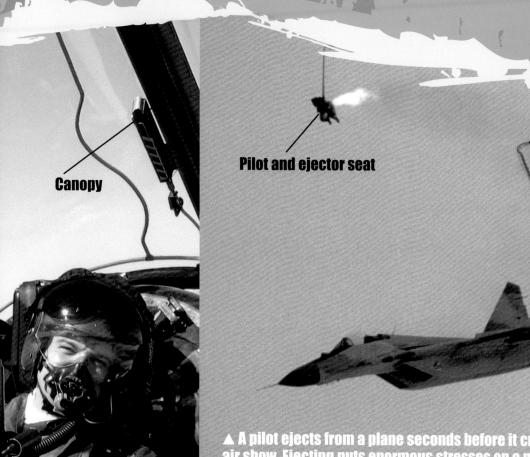

Canopy

Pilot and ejector seat

Cockpit canopy

▲ A pilot ejects from a plane seconds before it crashes at an air show. Ejecting puts enormous stresses on a pilot's body.

TRAINING FIGHTER PILOTS

The journey to the pilot's seat of a fighter jet is long and tough. Trainee fighter pilots face about four years of hard work, and only the best will succeed.

"At the Royal Air Force's fast-jet school students are taught how to fly in the Hawk. They learn how to fly using only the plane's instruments. This is so they can fly in zero visibility, for example in bad weather. They learn acrobatic flying and how to fly in formation with other aircraft. They also learn tactical formation maneuvering. This is when pilots fly and maneuver very close to each other. This is phase one of their training. It finishes with a 'Final Handling Test.' This test flight includes all the different types of flying the students have learned. They must pass this test before they can begin phase two."

Jules, UK Royal Air Force (RAF) Fast Jet Instructor

◄ United States Air Force (USAF) students train in T-38 Talons. After a training mission, USAF Captain Tony Brown uses T-38 models as he talks through the mission's maneuvers.

To be considered for fighter pilot training, you must have excellent exam results. You must also be physically fit and have perfect eyesight and above-average coordination skills.

▼ The Hawk F1 is the first jet aircraft that RAF fighter pilot trainees fly. Pilots say the Hawk handles well and is a lot of fun to fly.

"In phase 2 students learn how to 'fight' an aircraft. They learn how to drop bombs and strafe a target. This is when a pilot fires his weapons while flying low past his target. The students also learn how to intercept an enemy fighter plane and engage it in air-to-air combat.

To complete phase 2, students plan, brief, and lead a pair of aircraft on a low-level simulated attack. A simulated attack is a pretend mission that is made to feel as real as possible. During the mission there is the constant threat of an enemy attack. One of the school's experienced pilots acts as an enemy fighter."

Jules, RAF Fast Jet Instructor

G-FORCE

G-force is one of the most important things a pilot has to learn to cope with. G-force leaves trainee pilots feeling battered, bruised, and sick until they get used to the feeling.

The "g" in G-force stands for **"gravity."** The word "force" relates to acceleration—the change in speed that you feel. An object standing still on Earth's surface has acceleration of 1g. This is the force created by gravity pulling down on that object. Fighter pilots can sometimes experience 9g when they fly.

" As G-force increases it becomes difficult to breathe. This is because of the force pulling down on your rib cage and pushing it onto your lungs. The lack of air makes you feel very, very tired. The force drags all the blood in your body to your legs and feet. We wear special G-pants to keep this from happening. At around 6g your hearing starts to fade because there is not enough blood going to your brain. Next to go is peripheral vision. You can no longer see out of the corners of your eyes. It's like looking at the world through two toilet paper tubes.

Finally, everything turns black and white. More than this and you pass out. This is known as G-LOC. It stands for G-Induced Loss of Consciousness. Several pilots have been killed when they suffered G-LOC and crashed their planes. As the level of G-force decreases, your senses quickly return to normal. "

"Tomcat," USAF F-16 Pilot

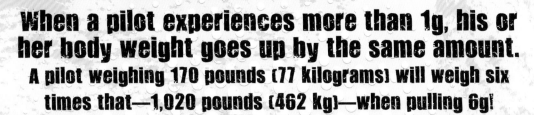

When a pilot experiences more than 1g, his or her body weight goes up by the same amount. A pilot weighing 170 pounds (77 kilograms) will weigh six times that—1,020 pounds (462 kg)—when pulling 6g!

▲ The effects of G-force show on this trainee fighter pilot's face as he pulls 6g.

"At low level, if the worst happened, we'd crash before we even had time to think about ejecting and that would mean certain death."

John, USAF F-16 Pilot

▲ An RAF Tornado F3 flies at low level over a lake.

LOW-LEVEL FLYING

Fighter pilots have to learn to fly at low level. Fighter planes must be able to "hug" the ground so that they can fly under enemy **radar** cover.

There's no **autopilot** or computer on the jet to handle this type of flying. The pilot reacts to the terrain (the land the plane is flying over) and flies using his or her skills and quick thinking.

> "Flying at low level is a skill that needs constant practice for us to stay current. It's exciting, dangerous, and requires immense focus.
>
> We'll be flying at around 500 miles per hour (800 kilometers per hour) at just 150 feet (45 meters) above the ground. At that speed, the world around you is a blur. We have to scan the terrain and react immediately to hills, mountains—whatever. We're traveling at seven miles (11 km) a minute so we have to think ahead. Navigating (finding your way) during high speed, low-level flying is one of the skills that trainee pilots have to learn."
>
> **John, USAF F-16 Pilot**

When flying at high altitudes, fighter jets often go supersonic. This means they fly faster than the speed of sound. The speed of sound, or Mach 1, is approximately 770 mph (1,240 km/h).

RAPTORS AND TYPHOONS

▲ Two USAF fighter pilots practice air-to-air combat maneuvers in F-22 Raptors.

Fighter jets are the most advanced aircraft in the world. The F-22 Raptor is a fighter jet in service with the United States Air Force (USAF). It is equipped for attack in the air and for bombing targets on the ground. It can fly at over 1,500 mph (2,400 km/h).

The F-22 Raptor uses **stealth technology** to make it almost invisible to the enemy. Stealth aircraft are able to make attacks before enemy radar can detect them.

▶ An RAF Typhoon F2 in flight.

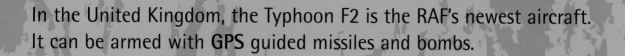

In the United Kingdom, the Typhoon F2 is the RAF's newest aircraft. It can be armed with **GPS** guided missiles and bombs.

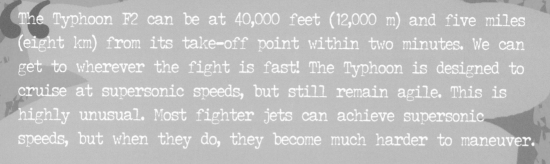

"The Typhoon F2 can be at 40,000 feet (12,000 m) and five miles (eight km) from its take-off point within two minutes. We can get to wherever the fight is fast! The Typhoon is designed to cruise at supersonic speeds, but still remain agile. This is highly unusual. Most fighter jets can achieve supersonic speeds, but when they do, they become much harder to maneuver.

The plane's computer sends information about fuel and altitude onto the visor of my helmet. This means I don't have to look down to check the cockpit instruments. I can carry out many functions by voice command. For me the Typhoon's most amazing innovation is its sight-activated missile firing system. I can fire missiles at a target simply by looking at it."

Matt, RAF Typhoon F2 Pilot

HARRIERS AND F-16s

The Harrier Jump Jet is a unique plane because it is able to make vertical takeoffs and landings. This makes it suitable for operations based on **aircraft carriers**.

▲ The Harrier Jump Jet in action—hovering above the ground (above) and taking off from the Royal Navy Aircraft Carrier HMS *Illustrious* (below).

▼ An F-16 drops a bomb. The plane's clear-view canopy gives the pilot 360° vision.

The F-16 fighter plane is known as the "Fighting Falcon." Its combat radius (the distance it can fly to the fight) is better than any other jet fighter. The F-16 can fly over 500 miles (800 km) to attack its target, defend itself against enemy fighters, deliver its missiles or bombs, and return to base.

F-16s are fitted with equipment known as sniper targeting pods. This equipment allows Forward Air Controllers (those on the ground who direct pilots to their targets) to see what the pilot sees before giving the "Cleared Hot" command to attack a ground target.

AIR-TO-AIR REFUELING

Modern fighter jets have to be light, fast, and agile. This means they can only carry enough fuel for 60 to 90 minutes of flying.

Fighter jets use afterburners to give them rapid acceleration. This is crucial in combat situations, but it increases the rate of fuel burn. Afterburners inject extra fuel into the engine to give the plane a sudden burst of thrust.

Fighter jets take on fuel from planes that act as airborne fuel tankers. Refueling in this way means that fighter jets can stay in the air and do not need to return to base to refuel.

"We have a nozzle on the side of our aircraft which has to connect with a basket at the end of a line on the tanker aircraft. I can only see the nozzle out of my peripheral vision. So the tanker is moving and the line from the tanker is also moving. The basket is moving, and so is my plane. I have to fly the end of the nozzle straight into the basket. It's a difficult maneuver and takes a lot of concentration!"

Eleanor, RAF Harrier Jump Jet Pilot

In combat situations, fighter jets that have been refueled fly alongside the tanker plane and protect it.

Line

Basket

Nozzle

▲ A UK Royal Air Force (RAF) Harrier GR9 takes on fuel from a United States Air Force (USAF) KC-10 Extender aircraft during a combat mission over Afghanistan. In this photo, the line from the KC-10 is shown connecting to a nozzle on the Harrier.

A FIGHTER PILOT'S DAY

Today, fighter pilots are busier than at any time since World War II. They are either training for war, on duty waiting to intercept a possible terrorist threat, or flying offensive operations in Afghanistan.

A typical training day usually includes weather briefings and a training mission called a sortie. The sortie usually lasts for about two hours.

"I still get a buzz from flying so I enjoy training sorties. They get us airborne and improve our skills.

A sortie might include flying in formation with three other aircraft. So you need to have really good control.

We might practice going in to a target ahead of the bombers. The bombers will be practicing dropping bombs onto a "bombing range" (like a firing range). Other fighter jets will be acting as enemy planes protecting the target (the bombing range). We will have to sneak up on the enemy fighters as if we were going to engage them and shoot them down. After the sortie you go to debrief. This is a meeting where you talk through what happened on the mission. If our bombers got to their targets and back safely it's a massive sense of achievement!"

Kat, RAF Tornado F3 Pilot

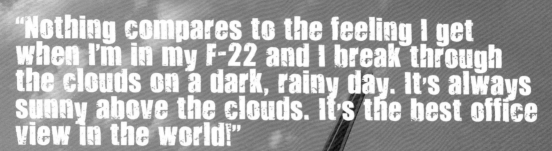

"Nothing compares to the feeling I get when I'm in my F-22 and I break through the clouds on a dark, rainy day. It's always sunny above the clouds. It's the best office view in the world!"

Brett, USAF F-22 Raptor Pilot

▼ Two USAF F-22 Raptors fly in formation as they undertake a training sortie.

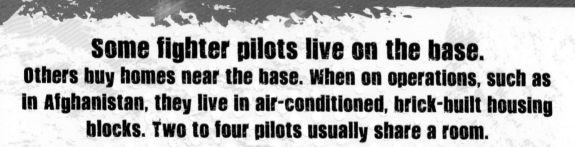

Some fighter pilots live on the base.

Others buy homes near the base. When on operations, such as in Afghanistan, they live in air-conditioned, brick-built housing blocks. Two to four pilots usually share a room.

QUICK REACTION ALERT

Fighter pilots on **Quick Reaction Alert (QRA)** duty are ready to deal with terrorist incidents involving planes.

Most countries in Europe and North America have QRA operations designed to defend their airspace. In the United Kingdom, for example, fighter controllers at an RAF base watch signals from aircraft. There can be thousands of aircraft flying in U.K. airspace at any time.

If any aircraft loses contact or is **hijacked**, the QRA fighter pilots are warned to "stand by." If a hostile plane were to enter U.K. airspace, QRA fighter pilots would be sent to intercept it.

▲ An RAF Tornado F3 pilot on QRA duty climbs into the cockpit.

If the call comes, every second counts. As the pilots run to their planes, the ground crews prepare them for rapid departure.

> "When we take off we're "weapons live." We have four radar-guided air-to-air missiles hung under the plane's fuselage. These missiles can be launched 20 miles (32 km) from our target. On the wings sit four heat-seeking air-to-air missiles and we have 180 rounds of high-explosive ammunition for the cannon."
>
> **QRA Pilot**

▼ An F3 Tornado climbs on afterburners to meet a threat in UK airspace.

During World War II, British fighter pilots waited,
fully outfitted, geared up, and ready to take to the air when
German aircraft entered Britain's airspace. This was known as
being ready to "scramble." Quick Reaction Alert (QRA) is the
modern-day version of scramble.

QRA IN ACTION

Within minutes of the call, the QRA jets are airborne. They climb on afterburners, accelerating at up to twice the speed of sound.

The pilots are ready to meet whatever threat is considered a danger.

Every QRA incident is tense. The fighter pilot's first task is to fly alongside the suspect aircraft. The pilots must assess the danger and report what is happening. They become the eyes of the decision maker on the ground.

▲ An Air Luxor 767 is escorted by RAF Tornado F3s as it lands on the Falkland Islands, in the Southern Atlantic Ocean. The islands house a large military base. Fighter jets practice intercepting and escorting airliners that visit the islands.

"We had one incident with a U.S. airliner that got airborne out of Heathrow Airport in London. There was another aircraft from the same airline taking off afterwards. Without contacting anybody, the pilot of the first aircraft did a circuit to wait for the other U.S. aircraft to catch up.

So, suddenly we had a worrying situation. An aircraft leaving London for the United States had carried out an unauthorized orbit and had turned back towards London. The airline pilot didn't answer his radio when called. To the guys on the ground it looked like a possible terrorist incident. We were scrambled to intercept.

We made visual contact with the airliner's pilot and signaled for him to talk on his radio. He explained he hadn't been hijacked and was allowed on his way. He would have been in trouble with his bosses when he landed!"

QRA pilot

QRA pilots work one day on and one day off.
Each "on duty" day lasts 24 hours. When the pilots rest during their 24 hours on duty, they sleep in their flying gear.

IN ACTION

Today, thousands of U.S. and U.K. military personnel are engaged in operations against the **Taliban** in Afghanistan. Andy is a Royal Air Force (RAF) Harrier pilot on duty in Afghanistan. Here, he describes his job, which is to protect forces on the ground:

"U.K. Royal Marines were clearing a village occupied by the Taliban. We were scrambled to support their operation. There were 26 compounds, or fortified buildings, in the village. I was given a diagram numbered one to 26 showing the position of each compound.

We were airborne in minutes. We checked in with the Forward Air Controller (FAC) by radio. The FAC is the man on the ground who tells us where he needs our fire power.

The FAC said, "We're taking heavy fire from compound number one and we're unable to move. I need a 1,000-pound bomb on that position."

My answer was, "Yes. In three minutes."

◄ A Harrier pilot ready for takeoff.

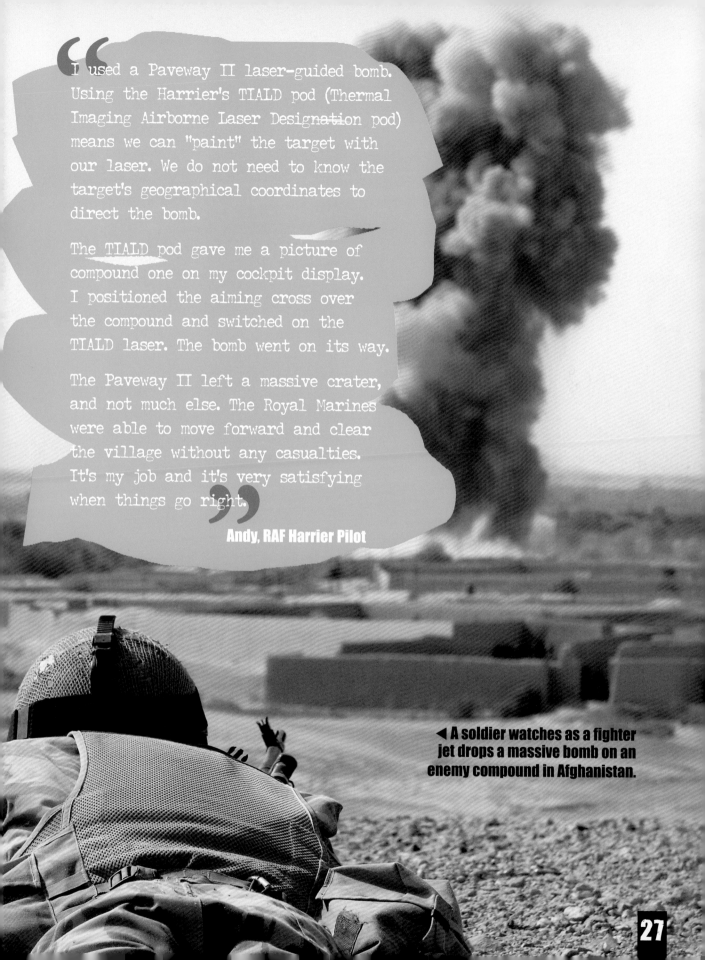

"I used a Paveway II laser-guided bomb. Using the Harrier's TIALD pod (Thermal Imaging Airborne Laser Designation pod) means we can "paint" the target with our laser. We do not need to know the target's geographical coordinates to direct the bomb.

The TIALD pod gave me a picture of compound one on my cockpit display. I positioned the aiming cross over the compound and switched on the TIALD laser. The bomb went on its way.

The Paveway II left a massive crater, and not much else. The Royal Marines were able to move forward and clear the village without any casualties. It's my job and it's very satisfying when things go right."

Andy, RAF Harrier Pilot

◄ A soldier watches as a fighter jet drops a massive bomb on an enemy compound in Afghanistan.

DANGER CLOSE

A fighter pilot's skills are never more crucial than when he or she is fighting "Danger Close." This means the pilot must drop bombs or fire missiles close to friendly forces. Here is how Andy tells it:

"This day we were providing support to some Canadian troops patrolling a village in Afghanistan. Suddenly, a small patrol on the edge of the village came under intense fire and couldn't move.

The Forward Air Controller (FAC) requested immediate support. I asked for an estimate of the position of friendly forces in relation to the enemy. He came back with 300 feet (91 m)."

Sometimes fighter pilots simply use a "show of force" to scare enemy fighters into retreat. A fighter jet flying at 500 mph (800 km/h) just 100 feet (30 m) above the ground is a terrifying sight!

"That's "Danger Close." A large bomb would affect everyone in the immediate area, including friendly troops. I would have to use CRV-7 rockets. I asked the FAC to throw up a smoke bomb so I could be sure of his position.

I positioned for a rocket attack starting from 18,000 feet (5,500 m). This height gave me good visibility and a steep angle for my attack dive which minimizes the spread of the rockets. I tipped into a steep dive and got ready to hit the "pickle button" and fire the CRV-7s. The rockets travel at three times the speed of sound.

The first strike scored a direct hit. The FAC radioed me, "Direct hit, but we're still taking fire from one or two fighters." So we came in for a repeat attack, and all the firing stopped.

Afterwards, I found out that the Canadian troops had needed to reposition even closer to the Taliban position. They were actually less than 100 feet (30 m) from where my rockets landed."

Andy, RAF Harrier Pilot

▲ An F-16 fires a Maverick rocket.

IT'S A FACT!

Fighter pilots fly for either the air force or the navy. The majority of fighter pilots are part of the air force. Both air force and navy pilots do the same dangerous job, fly the same aircraft, and receive the same training.

The United States Air Force (USAF) has over 6,000 aircraft in service. Over 330,000 men and women work for the USAF.

The U.K.'s Royal Air Force (RAF) currently operates over 1,000 aircraft. Over 42,000 men and women work for the RAF. Their jobs include pilots, mechanics, air traffic controllers, cooks, and medics.

Fighter pilots on duty in Afghanistan live at the Kandahar base. Thousands of soldiers and pilots from around the world live here. There are gyms, internet cafes, and churches on the base. There is even a Pizza Hut and a Subway restaurant!

Only one in every 40 hopefuls makes it into pilot training with the U.K.'s Royal Air Force (RAF). The RAF spends over one million pounds (about 1.5 million dollars) to train each new recruit.

Fighter pilots online
www.airforce.com
www.raf.mod.uk

GLOSSARY

aircraft carrier A ship that functions as an air base at sea. The largest ships in any navy, carriers can hold up to 85 aircraft and a crew of 3,200 per carrier.

autopilot An automated system that can control, navigate, and even, in some cases, land a plane according to programmed instructions.

Forward Air Controller A soldier on the ground who tells fighter aircraft pilots where their firepower is needed.

G-force The force, experienced by a fighter pilot when flying at high speed, caused by the forces of acceleration and gravity pushing and pulling on the body.

G-pants Special pants with pouches that inflate with air when the pilot experiences G-force, constricting the flow of blood to the legs and feet.

GPS (Global Positioning System) A system of satellites that allows users to figure out the location, direction, and speed of themselves or others.

gravity The force that attracts objects toward Earth.

hijack To take control of a vehicle or aircraft using force or violence.

navigation The process of planning and finding a route from one place to another.

Quick Reaction Alert (QRA) The name given to the system of defending airspace from potential threats. Pilots, aircraft, and ground crews are ready to scramble on a 10-minute standby.

radar A way of detecting distant objects. Radar can determine an object's position and speed by sending radio waves that reflect off the object's surface.

stealth technology Technology that makes an aircraft almost invisible to radar. This is done with the use of panels that absorb rather than reflect radar waves.

Taliban A radical Sunni Muslim organization that governed Afghanistan from 1996 to 2001. It has been fighting a guerrilla war against the current government of Afghanistan and allied forces.

terrorist A person who tries to frighten people or governments into doing what he or she wants by using violence or the threat of violence.

INDEX

A

Afghanistan 5, 19, 20, 21, 26, 27, 28, 30, 31
afterburners 18, 23, 24
air traffic controllers 30
air-to-air missiles 23
air-to-air refuelling 18
aircraft carriers 16, 17, 31
autopilot 13, 31

B

bombs 4, 9, 14, 15, 17, 20, 26, 27, 28, 29

C

combat situations 4, 6, 7, 9, 14, 17, 18, 19, 26, 28, 29
CRV-7 rockets 29

D

Danger Close 28, 29
dangers 4, 8, 9

E

ejecting 6, 7

F

F-16s 4, 29
F-22 Raptors 14, 21
Fighting Falcons
see F-16s
flares 5
Forward Air Controllers 17, 26, 28, 29, 31

G

G-force 6, 10, 11, 31
G-LOC 10
G-pants 10, 31
GPS 15, 31

H

Harrier jump jets 5, 16, 17, 19, 26
Hawk F1 8
heat-seeking missiles 5, 23

K

Kandahar base 30
KC-10 Extender aircraft 19

L

living conditions 21, 30
low-level flying 9, 12, 13

Q

Quick Reaction Alert (QRA) 22, 23, 24, 25, 31

R

radar 13, 14, 31
Royal Air Force (RAF) 6, 8, 9, 12, 14, 15, 19, 22, 24, 30

S

scramble 23
sight-activated missile firing system 15
sniper targeting pods 17
sorties 20, 21
speed of sound 13, 24, 29
stealth technology 14, 31
supersonic flying 13, 15

T

T-38 Talons 8
Taliban 26, 31
tanker planes 18, 19
terrorists 5, 20, 22, 25, 31
TIALD pod 27
Tornado F3s 6, 12, 22, 23, 24
training 4, 8, 9, 10, 13, 20, 21, 30
Typhoon F2s 14, 15

U

United States Air Force (USAF) 8, 14, 19, 21, 30

Printed in the USA—BG